Leading Lady

HILLARY RODHAM CLINTON

Written by Julie Bach

Published by Abdo & Daughters, 4940 Viking Drive Suite 622, Edina, Minnesota 55435.

Library bound edition distributed by Rockbottom Books, Pentagon Tower, P.O. Box 36036, Minneapolis, Minnesota 55435.

Photo Credits: Bettmann pgs. 15, 17, 19, 21, 24, 27, 29
                  Black Star pgs. cover, 5, 7, 10

Edited by Rosemary Wallner

LIBRARY OF CONGRESS CATALOGING-IN-PUBLICATION DATA
Bach, Julie S., 1963-
    Hillary Clinton / written by Julie Bach.
        p. cm. — (Leading Ladies)
        Includes bibliographical references (p.) and index.
Summary: A biography of Hillary Rodham Clinton which focuses on her childhood, education, work as a lawyer, and involvement in her husband's political career.
    ISBN 1-56239-221-2
    1. Clinton, Hillary Rodham -- Juvenile literature. 2. Clinton, Bill, 1946-   -- Juvenile literature. 3. Presidents -- United States -- Wives -- Biography -- Juvenile literature. [1. Clinton, Hillary Rodham. 2. First Ladies.] I. Title. II. Series.
E887.C55B33   1993   973.929'092--dc20   93-15325
                            [B]

TABLE OF CONTENTS

AN ENERGETIC WOMAN

It is midnight in Wisconsin. A group of tired people are riding a bus through the darkness. Before dawn, they will stop in a small town to talk to hundreds of cheering supporters. Most of the people on the bus are asleep, but one woman and man are awake, earnestly talking.

The man and woman on the bus are Bill and Hillary Clinton.

In 1992, they traveled throughout the United States as Bill campaigned for president. As the campaign went on, the country became fascinated with Hillary. Some people even suggested that she should run for president.

Who is this energetic woman—mother, lawyer, and children's advocate? How did she come to be a part of this race for the most prestigious job in America?

*The Clintons and the Gores travelling by bus through the U.S.
during the campaign for president, 1992.*

A SECURE CHILDHOOD

Hillary Rodham was born on October 26, 1947. Her father, Hugh Rodham, owned a small textile company. Her mother, Dorothy Rodham, had left college to marry and raise a family.

After Hillary was born, the Rodhams had two other children, Hugh, Jr., and Tony.

When Hillary was four years old, her family moved to Park Ridge, Illinois, a suburb of Chicago. Hillary liked her new home, except for the neighborhood bully, a girl named Suzy.

Nearly every day, Suzy hit Hillary and sent her sprawling. For weeks Hillary went home to her mother complaining about the bully. Finally, Dorothy Rodham told Hillary to stand up for herself. Hillary went outside and knocked Suzy down. She ran back to her mother, proud of her victory.

Hillary had many other victories. She was an ambitious and smart child. She was a Brownie and a Girl Scout and earned every badge. She and her brothers played word games and rarely watched television.

Hillary Rodham Clinton as a teenager.

In 1961, Hillary was fourteen years old. She wrote to the National Aeronautics and Space Administration (NASA). She wrote that she wanted to become an astronaut. But officials at NASA told her that girls were not allowed to be astronauts.

Hillary had never been told she could not do something because she was a girl. Her parents, she said, "gave me my belief in working hard, doing well in school, and not being limited by the fact that I was a girl."

As she grew up, Hillary worked hard at sports. She was not a star athlete, but she always did her best. Competition taught her some good lessons about life. "You win one day, you lose the next day, you don't take it personally. You get up every day and you go on," she says.

The Rodham family attended a Methodist church. There, at an early age, Hillary learned about caring for other people. She organized clothes drives and a carnival to help migrant workers. Sometimes she took care of migrant workers' children while their parents worked in the fields.

In high school, Hillary's youth minister taught her other ways to help people. He took the church youth group to poor neighborhoods on the South Side of Chicago. There they made friends with black and Hispanic teenagers. They talked about ideas and read poetry. Hillary helped give these teenagers hope for a better life.

A GROWING COMMITMENT

Hillary graduated from Maine South High School in 1965 with honors. In the fall she went to Wellesley College, a women's school in Massachusetts. She was president of her college government and an honor student. Classmates and professors remember how hard Hillary studied. They said that she would rather talk about politics than go to a football game or ride a bike.

Hillary graduated from college in 1969. Her classmates chose her to give a speech at their commencement. Hillary talked about young people in the 1960s. They wanted a different life than their parents had lived, she said. They wanted to help change the world. The speech was so good that *Life* magazine wrote an article about it. Hillary's picture was in the magazine.

*Hillary Rodham Clinton at Wellesley College giving
her graduating class's commencement speech, 1969.*

Hillary went to graduate school at Yale Law School in Connecticut. She wanted to be a lawyer, and she also wanted to help people. She especially wanted to help children. Hillary studied the legal rights of poor children. She worked at the Yale Child Study Center.

While at law school, Hillary learned about the Children's Defense Fund (CDF). This group tries to win legal cases that will help children and poor people have a better life. Through the CDF, Hillary became even more committed to helping children.

THE YOUNG MAN FROM ARKANSAS

At law school, one of Hillary's classmates was a young man from Arkansas named Bill Clinton. Bill liked Hillary, but he was scared to talk to her. He stared at her in class and around campus. One evening in the library, Hillary stood up and walked over to him. "Look," she said, "if you're going to keep staring at me, then I'm going to keep looking back, and I think we ought to know each other's names. I'm Hillary Rodham." Bill Clinton was so stunned that he forgot his name.

Bill and Hillary liked each other right away, but Bill was nervous about falling in love with Hillary. He knew she was going to be a successful lawyer. She would probably work in an important law firm in a big city when she graduated. But he wanted to go back to Arkansas. He wanted to help the people he had grown up with. He was sure Hillary would never move to Arkansas.

A HARD DECISION

Hillary and Bill both graduated from law school in 1973. Bill returned to Arkansas. Hillary worked for a short time at the Children's Defense Fund in Cambridge, Massachusetts.

Later that summer, Hillary went to Washington, D.C., to work on a committee. The committee was trying to find out whether President Richard Nixon had committed a crime while he was in office. The committee had a very serious job to do.

In August, Nixon resigned. The committee had uncovered Nixon's wrongdoing. Hillary was proud of the work she had done, but her job in Washington was over. Where would she go now? she asked herself.

Law firms in big cities like New York and Chicago were offering her good jobs. But Bill was in Arkansas, and she wanted to be with him. What would she do?

Hillary decided to follow her heart. She moved to Fayetteville, a town in northwest Arkansas. There she and Bill taught at the University of Arkansas Law School. Her family and friends thought she was crazy. They liked Bill, but they thought Hillary belonged in a big eastern city where she could be a powerful lawyer.

After a year, Hillary wondered what she might be missing. She wasn't sure she wanted to spend the rest of her life in Arkansas. She traveled to Chicago, Boston, Washington, and New York. But her work in Fayetteville was more interesting than anything she saw in these cities. She decided to go back.

Bill met her at the airport. He drove her to a small house that she had once admired. Bill was so happy that Hillary was coming back to Arkansas, he had bought the house. "So you're going to have to marry me," he told her when she saw it. Two months later, in October 1975, she did.

THE GOVERNOR'S WIFE

Shortly after they were married, Bill was elected attorney general of Arkansas. The Clintons moved to Little Rock, the state capital. Hillary joined the Rose Law Firm, one of the largest in the state. Then, in 1978, Bill was elected governor of Arkansas. He was the youngest governor in the country.

Hillary worked hard at the Rose Law Firm. Twice during her career there she was named one of the country's top one hundred lawyers. She also sat on the board of directors for the Children's Defense Fund and many other organizations.

Hillary was happy with her life as a successful lawyer. She was happy that Bill was the governor. But many Arkansas voters did not like Hillary. They considered her an outsider because she was from Chicago. They disapproved of her keeping her own last name, Rodham, instead of taking her husband's name.

Hillary had never worried about what other people thought of her. She had always done what she believed was right. But two years later Bill lost the election for governor. Part of the reason he lost was that the voters didn't like the governor's wife.

Bill Clinton being sworn in for his first term as governor of Arkansas in Little Rock, 1979. His wife, Hillary, stands by him.

Hillary felt his loss was unfair. But she also felt that he might lose again if she did not make some changes. She decided to compromise. She would change her name to Hillary Rodham Clinton. She would adopt some southern ways. But she would not change who she was. She certainly would not give up her job as a lawyer.

For the next two years, Hillary and Bill traveled throughout Arkansas. They campaigned as hard as they could. In 1982, their work paid off. Bill was reelected governor.

One other change in Hillary's life occurred between the two elections. She became a mother. Chelsea Victoria, Hillary and Bill's only child, was born in 1980.

CRUSADING FOR EDUCATION

Soon after Bill Clinton was reelected governor, he appointed Hillary to head a committee. The committee's job was to improve education in Arkansas. Hillary visited every county in the state. She talked to teachers, principals, and superintendents.

*Hillary becomes a mother. Chelsea Victoria,
Hillary and Bill's only child, was born in 1980.*

17

After a lot of hard work, Hillary and Bill persuaded the state congress to pass new laws. The laws made classes in Arkansas schools smaller. They created standard graduation requirements for high school students. They required that teachers take tests to make sure they were qualified to teach.

Many people in Arkansas complained about Hillary's role on the committee. They thought the governor should not appoint his wife to such an important job. Also, many people did not like the new laws. One school librarian called Hillary "lower than a snake's belly."

But Hillary didn't mind the criticism. She knew the new laws would help children in her state get a good education. Bill Clinton remained governor of Arkansas. Then, during the summer of 1987, he thought about running for president of the United States.

It would be a big challenge. Bill and Hillary would have to campaign together. They would be away from Chelsea, who was seven. They decided against it.

*Hillary Rodham Clinton believes strongly in education. Here she
visits her old high school to talk about reforms the new
administration plans to make.*

THE CAMPAIGN FOR PRESIDENT

Four years later, in 1991, Bill Clinton again thought about running for president. Chelsea was older now. Bill and Hillary felt she could handle the pressure of a national campaign.

One morning, Hillary woke up. She looked over at her husband. "You almost have to do it," she said. "Do you have any idea what we're getting into?" he replied. "I know," Hillary answered. "It'll be tough." But Hillary had no idea just how tough it would be.

Soon after Bill declared his candidacy, rumors surfaced about their marriage. When Bill had lost the race for governor in 1980, he had been depressed, and he had been unfaithful to Hillary. Reporters found out about his infidelity. Hillary and Bill admitted that their marriage had been through some rough times. But, they explained, they had stayed together because they loved each other. Their marriage was fine now.

That was just the beginning. Soon someone criticized Hillary for having a career. People began to say that she had neglected her family. This rumor hurt Hillary deeply. She was devoted to her family. She had never felt that her career kept her from being a good mother and wife.

Hillary was an agressive campaigner for her husband.
Because of this she's often criticized.

Then people criticized Hillary for being too liberal. They said her political views would destroy America's values. They tried to portray Hillary as a woman without values. But Hillary knew this was also a lie. She was devoted to her family and her country. She believed in being honest and standing up for the truth. All her life she had tried to help people, especially children. She felt helping people was the best value she could have.

The attacks went on. People criticized her personality. They criticized the way she wore her hair. They criticized some of her friends. Hillary remained calm. She never attacked the people who tried to hurt her. She wanted more than anything to help solve America's problems. She tried to focus on the good she and Bill could do if he was elected.

Many people supported Hillary during the campaign. Hillary loved talking to people on the campaign bus trips around the country. They talked about their hopes for themselves and for the nation. One woman said she put off her treatment for cancer just so she could meet Hillary. Another woman said to Hillary, "Please don't lose heart."

Wherever Hillary went, people were impressed with her. She gave great speeches. She answered questions honestly. She talked to children and showed she cared about them. She never seemed to tire, even after long days on the bus and nights of little sleep.

TAKING CARE OF HER FAMILY

Throughout the campaign, Hillary always thought of Chelsea. She worked hard to make sure Chelsea felt loved and secure. She called Chelsea on the phone every day. They talked about homework and many other things.

Every few days Hillary flew home to be with Chelsea. The day before the final presidential debate in Michigan, Hillary slipped away. She spent the entire day with her daughter. "The most important thing in my life is my family," she said.

Family has always been important to Hillary. When the Clintons lived in Arkansas, Hillary hardly ever missed one of Chelsea's dance performances or ball games. Every weekend she dismissed the staff of the Governor's Mansion. She wanted her family to spend time alone together.

Chelsea joined her parents for the campaign just a few times. Here the whole family celebrates with supporters at the Democratic National Convention, July 1992.

Chelsea is a bright and athletic girl. She plays volleyball and softball. She especially likes dance. Her name comes from "Chelsea Morning," a song that Bill and Hillary liked.

Hillary kept Chelsea out of the campaign as much as possible. Chelsea stayed in Arkansas while Bill and Hillary traveled. Her grandparents took care of her. Hillary asked reporters not to bother the young girl. Chelsea joined her parents for the campaign just a few times.

In November 1992, the whole family celebrated when Bill Clinton won the election. The campaign had been hard on them.

Now they could look forward to moving into the White House. The Clinton family began to make plans for their new life.

Meanwhile, Americans wondered what kind of a president's wife Hillary would be.

A NEW KIND OF FIRST LADY

The president's wife is called the First Lady. The First Lady hosts events at the White House. She entertains guests from other countries. She is expected to support her husband and to help special causes.

In Arkansas, Hillary had broken many traditions as a governor's wife. She worked full time, served on an important committee, and spoke her mind. Throughout the campaign for president, Hillary and Bill had described their marriage as a partnership. Will that partnership continue in the White House?

Soon after the inauguration, Bill put Hillary in charge of a commission. This commission's job is to improve health care in America. Many Americans do not have health insurance and they cannot afford to see a doctor when they are sick.

Some Americans thought the president's wife should not have such an important job. Others were happy that Hillary could help the country. A month after she was put in charge of the commission, most Americans agreed that she was doing a good job.

First Lady Hillary Rodham Clinton (L) with President-elect Bill Clinton, Vice President Gore, and Tipper Gore during a victory celebration in Little Rock, November 3, 1992.

Hillary has said that while she's in the White House she wants to help children. She wants fewer children to be poor. She wants all children to get a good education. And she wants all children to get good health care, including immunization shots.

Other First Ladies worked for causes and influenced politics. Edith Wilson was the wife of the twenty-eighth president. Some people say she ran the government after her husband had a stroke. Eleanor Roosevelt was the wife of the thirty-second president. She spoke out for civil rights and women's equality. And Rosalynn Carter, the wife of the thirty-ninth president, often sat in on cabinet meetings.

But Hillary is different from even these women. She represents a new generation in the White House. She is a career woman and a mother. She is a feminist who believes in traditional values. She is devoted to her husband, and she is his equal partner. Whatever Hillary does in the White House, she will be an exciting First Lady to watch.

Hillary Rodham Clinton, First Lady, represents a new generation in the White House.

GLOSSARY

Advocate - A person that defends or maintains a cause or proposal.

Astronaut - A person who travels beyond the Earth's atmosphere.

Attorney General - A person in a court of law who is legally qualified to prosecute and defend actions in the court.

Campaign - A connected series of operations designed to bring about a particular result.

Children's Defense Fund - A group that tries to win legal cases that will help children and poor people have a better life.

Commencement speech - The ceremonial speech for conferring degrees or diplomas.

Congress - The supreme legislative body of a nation.

Election - The right, power or privilege of making a choice.

First Lady - The wife of a chief executive of a country.

Governor - A person that exercises authority over an area or a group.

Hispanic - Relating to the people, speech or culture of Spain.

Inauguration - A ceremonial induction into office.

Lawyer - A person whose profession is to conduct lawsuits for clients or to advise as to legal rights.

Liberal - A person who is open-minded or not strict in the observance of orthodox, traditional or established ways.

Migrant workers - A person who moves regularly in order to find work, mostly in harvesting crops.

NASA - National Aeronautics and Space Administration.

Politics - The art or science of government.

REFERENCES

Abbott, Shirley. "Hillary Speaks to Her Mythologizers." Glamour, August 1992.

Anthony, Carl Sferrazza. "Hillary Clinton: What I hope to Do as First Lady." Good Houskeeping, January 1993.

Carlson, Margaret. "A Different Kind of First Lady." Time, Nov. 16, 1992.

Carlson, Margaret. "The Dynamic Duo" Time, Jan. 4, 1993.

Chua-Eoan, Howard G., "First Friends." People, Nov. 16,1992.

Clift, Eleanor. "Hillary's Ultimate Juggling Act." Newsweek, Nov. 16, 1992.

Cooper, Matthew. "The Hillary Factor." U.S. News & World Report, April 27, 1992.

"Hillary Clinton Reveals Black College Grad Helped Direct and Shape Her Career." Jet, Nov. 2, 1992.

INDEX